C0-AAV-716

On Loss

by Jack Bielan

ISBN 1-55366-271-7

Published by Stewart House Publishing Inc.
290 North Queen Street, Suite 210
Etobicoke, Ontario M9C 5K4 Canada

www.stewarthousepub.com

Executive Vice President and Publisher: Ken Proctor
Director of Publishing and Product Acquisition: Joe March
Production Manager: Ruth Bradley-St-Cyr

Copy Editor: Susan Paterson
Book design: Laura Ciruls/Hume Imaging
Printed and bound in Canada at Transcontinental Printing

Over the past few years, in my quest for answers to seemingly unanswerable questions about the loss of loved ones, I have consulted with a variety of scholars and major thinkers.

I've sought the counsel of learned pastors, rabbis, priests, a lama and the elders of a Mormon church.

I've spoken with teachers, psychologists, bookstore owners, street-corner philosophers and Starbucks malingerers. I've learned from common and not-so-common people who have somehow found meaning in the face of tragedy.

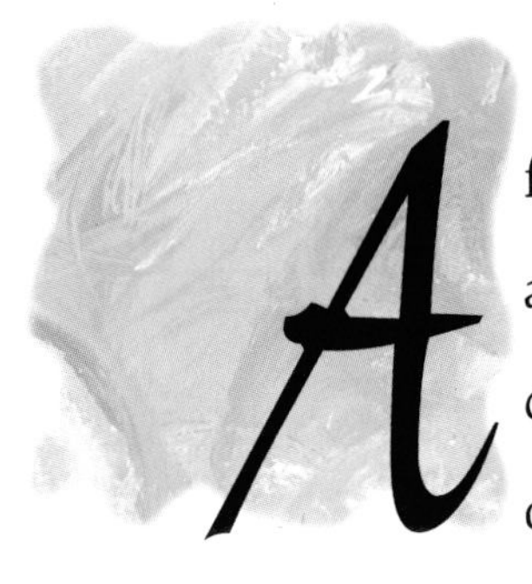

After processing all this assorted input, I have come to formulate my own opinions about some aspects of loss. Among them is an affirmation that, to some extent, death is an illusion.

Don't get me wrong: God knows that I'm certainly not one to deny the utterly immeasurable pain and agony of losing cherished loved ones. For some of us, we may allow that pain to become so overwhelming that it can ultimately cripple or destroy us.

But at some point in this worst-of-all process, if we find the courage to momentarily set aside our grief, can we allow ourselves to ask a crucial, against-the-grain question:

Is it truly logical to believe that all the goodness, kindness, wisdom and courage; all the unconditional caring, compassion, friendship and love – intrinsic ingredients which comprise the souls of those whom we have held so dear – does it really make sense that such Divinely-created creatures, possessing such extraordinary components, would altogether cease to exist – simply because their physical bodies stop functioning?

Call it wishful thinking if you want, but for me: I just don't think so.

Considering all the exquisite and wondrous elements of this world, I find it hard to believe that a God capable of creating such majesty; One who would craft all these miraculous colors and textures and scientifically-unexplainable phenomena - could actually be so short-sighted as to create souls which are capable of so much - only to abandon their existence because of the frailty of their marvellous, yet so desperately fragile, bodies.

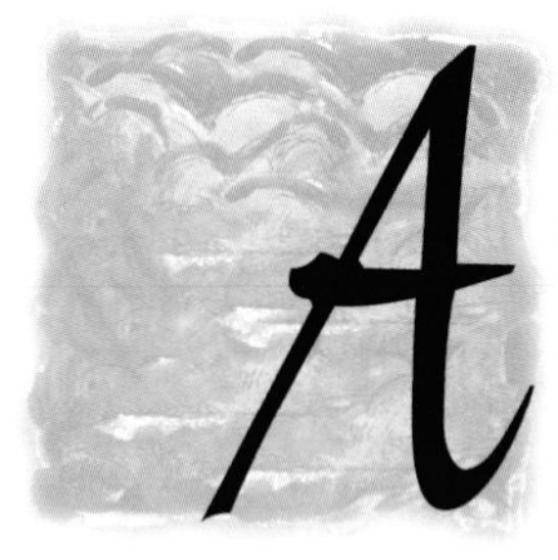

s a way of forging a personal truce with this dilemma, I've come up with a rather simplistic analogy about death.

When I was a child, my mother would sometimes take me shopping at the May Company

Wilshire in Los Angeles. I have fond memories of those times, which probably explains why I find some real comfort in childishly likening "existence" to a department store.

I respectfully suggest that this life of ours is like the first floor of the May Company Wilshire. There are an infinite variety of sights, smells and departments from which to choose, and we soon go our separate ways and experience our individual journeys.

owever, at some given point - different for each of us but unavoidable for all of us - we have to get on the elevator and go to the next floor.

I've also learned that, despite their assorted differences, most major religions and philosophies do seem to generally agree on one issue: our souls and everything we've learned – *truly don't stop when we pass away.*

In department stores terms: we simply ascend to the mezzanine where, among assorted holy encounters, we hopefully get to learn a lot more about the real Big Picture.

ut now another question arises: what are the responsibilities of those of us who are left – we, whose turns have yet to arrive? It's all well and good for all those departed souls to find enrichment and enlightenment, but what about us who are still here, trying to get through today?

Speaking only for myself, I've drawn a few conclusions and established some wishful priorities.

At the top of the list is my hope that, when the time comes and my personal elevator door is about to close, I'm able to look back and forward with peace in my heart.

I'll want to know that I've adequately communicated to dear friends and cherished loved ones the full depth of what they mean to me and how much they've brought to my life – and that I'm timidly banking on the belief that our separation is only temporary.

I also hope to tell my dear ones with whom I'm joyously reunited that I didn't dwell in self-pity any longer than necessary – but instead honored them by finding ways to make my life its most meaningful in their physical absence.

I'd like them to recognize that I didn't waste precious time, and I pray that they'll have been proud of me. And I'll want them to know that I used their love for me as my best strength when I was at my most weak.

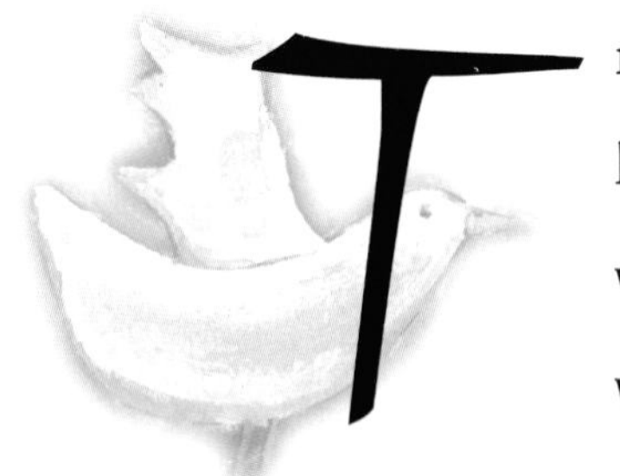

Truth to be known, in our heart of hearts we all know what our departed loved ones' wishes are for us.

They want us to flourish.

They want us to embrace life and our family and friends even more than before.

They'd like us to recognize our opportunities and acknowledge our achievements. They'd love to see us fully utilize our creativity and talents, along with our individual gifts and all our God-given abilities.

They want us to make each day a lifetime and they expect us to find the courage to rise to our own levels of greatness with honesty, integrity and a sense of service to others.

They'd also be very happy to see us smile – a lot.

And they want us to know that we're never really alone if we embrace the God who truly loves us and we live by God's laws and commandments.

And maybe, whenever we feel the need to do so, they'd like us to find a private moment to quietly sit and talk with them – just as we always have.

And if we listen closely enough… softly enough… we'll know that it *is* true: they may have gone to the next floor – but they haven't left the building.

And they're not lost to us. Not really.

That's certainly what they want for us.

No doubt about it.

The Serenity Prayer

God grant me the Serenity to accept the
things I cannot change...

Courage to change the things I can...

And Wisdom to know the difference.

Living one day at a time,

Enjoying one moment at a time,

Accepting hardship as the pathway to peace.

Taking, as He did, this sinful world as it is, not as I would have it.

Trusting that He will make all
things right if I surrender to His will.

That I may be reasonably
happy in this life.

And supremely happy with Him
forever in the next.

Amen.